Mel Bay Presents

Songs of Peace & Friendship

By Jerry Silverman

Contents

Friendship
Freundschaft
3-part round

The great German composer Ludwig van Beethoven (1770–1827) wrote many monumental compositions for orchestras, instrumental ensembles and voices. He felt strongly about individual liberty and freedom of conscience. He was also able to express most basic human emotions in compositions like this simple three-part round. On page 28 you will find one of his most famous compositions, "Ode To Joy."

By Ludwig van Beethoven

Everybody Loves Saturday Night

In the 1950s, when Nigeria was still a British colony, the authorities imposed a curfew on the people in an attempt to curtail the independence movement. For some reason, the curfew was not imposed on Saturday nights. This simple song grew out of the joy of the people who were permitted to enjoy themselves at least one night of the week. It has been picked up and sung in many languages all over the world. Can you sing it in any other language?

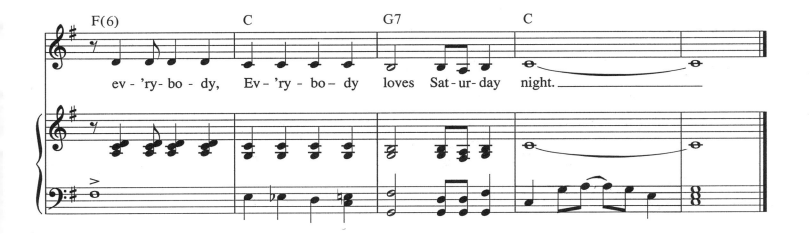

ev - 'ry- bo- dy, Ev - 'ry - bo - dy loves Sat - ur - day night. _____

Nigerian:
(original language)

Bobo waro fero Satodeh,
Bobo waro fero Satodeh.
Bobo waro, bobo waro,
Bobo waro, bobo waro,
Bobo waro fero Satodeh.

French:

Tout le monde aime Samedi soir,
Tout le monde aime Samedi soir.
Tout le monde, tout le monde,
Tout le monde, tout le monde,
Tout le monde aime Samedi soir.

Yiddish:

Yeder eyner hot lieb Shabas ba nacht,
Yeder eyner hot lieb Shabas ba nacht.
Yeder eyner, yeder eyner,
Yeder eyner, yeder eyner,
Yeder eyner hot lieb Shabas ba nacht.

Chinese:

Ren ren si huan li pai lu,
Ren ren si huan li pai lu.
Ren ren si, ren ren si,
Ren ren si, ren ren si,
Ren ren si huan li pai lu.

Russian:

Fsiem nravitsa subbota vietcher,
Fsiem nravitsa subbota vietcher.
Fsiem nravitsa, fsiem nravitsa,
Fsiem nravitsa, fsiem nravitsa,
Fsiem nravitsa subbota vietcher.

Czech:

Kazhdi ma rad sabotu vietcher,
Kazhdi ma rad sabotu vietcher.
Kazhdi ma, kazhdi ma,
Kazhdi ma, kazhdi ma,
Kazhdi ma rad sabotu vietcher.

Spanish:

A todos le gusta la noche del Sabado,
A todos le gusta la noche del Sabado,
A todos le gusta, a todos le gusta,
A todos le gusta, a todos le gusta,
A todos le gusta la noche del Sabado.

"American"

All the cats dig Saturday night the most,
All the cats dig Saturday night the most,
All the cats, all the cats,
All the cats, all the cats,
All the cats dig Saturday night the most.

Come And Go With Me

Come and go with me to that land, Come and go with me to that

land, Come and go with me to that land where I'm bound. _____

_____ Come and go with me to that land, Come and go with me to that

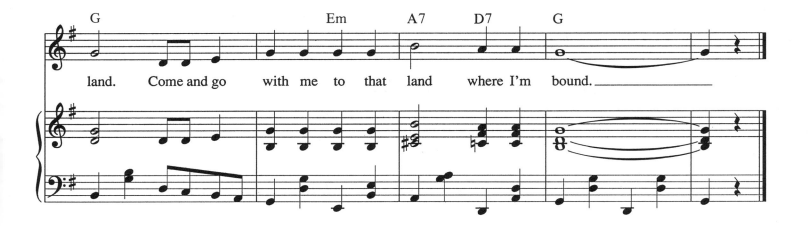

There ain't no bowing in that land, ain't no bowing in that land,
Ain't no bowing in that land where I'm bound.
There ain't no bowing in that land, ain't no bowing in that land,
Ain't no bowing in that land where I'm bound.

There ain't no kneeling in that land, ain't no kneeling in that land,
Ain't no kneeling in that land where I'm bound.
There ain't no kneeling in that land, ain't no kneeling in that land,
Ain't no kneeling in that land where I'm bound.

There's peace and freedom in that land, peace and freedom in that land,
Peace and freedom in that land where I'm bound.
There's peace and freedom in that land, peace and freedom in that land,
Peace and freedom in that land where I'm bound.

Repeat Verse One

Down By The Riverside

I'm gon - na lay down my sword and shield, Down by the river - side, ___ Down by the river - side, ___ Down by the river - side. ___ Gon - na lay down my sword and shield, Down by the river - side, ___ And stu - dy war no more.

I'm gonna put on my long white robe,
Down by the riverside,
Down by the riverside,
Down by the riverside.
I'm gonna put on my long white robe,
Down by the riverside,
And study war no more. *Chorus*

I'm gonna talk with the Prince of Peace,
Down by the riverside,
Down by the riverside,
Down by the riverside.
I'm gonna talk with the Prince of Peace,
Down by the riverside,
And study war no more. *Chorus*

I'm gonna join hands with everyone,
Down by the riverside,
Down by the riverside,
Down by the riverside.
I'm gonna join hands with everyone,
Down by the riverside,
And study war no more.   *Chorus*

This Little Light Of Mine

shine, Ev-'ry day, ev-'ry day, ev-'ry day, ev-'ry day, ev-'ry day, _____ Gon-na let my lit-tle light shine. _____ On Mon-day He gave me the gift of love, On Tues-day peace came from a-bove, On

Fine

Candy

Al Wood wrote this song in 1952 from the point of view of a child whose brother was fighting in Korea.

By Albert Wood

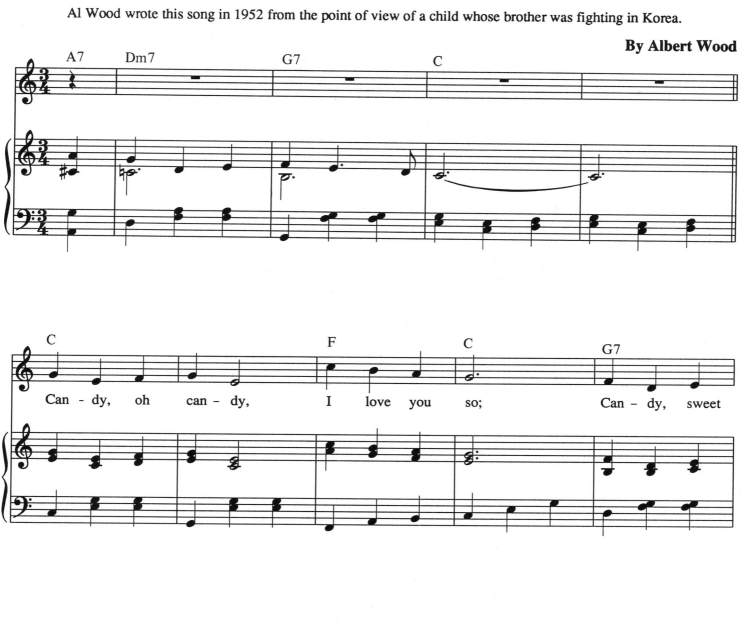

Can - dy, oh can - dy, I love you so; Can - dy, sweet can - dy, Please don't go. You once was a pen - ny, but

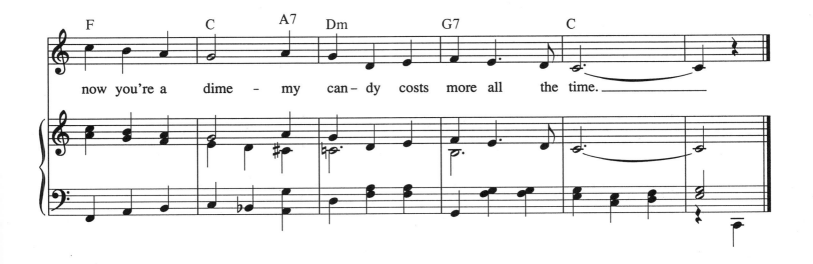

now you're a dime – my can-dy costs more all the time.

I took you to school with me every day,
And you were with me when I went to play,
I then could afford you, things were so fine,
My candy costs more all the time.

I'll wrap you in paper and save you today,
Some for big brother who's so far away;
He's gone off to war, this brother of mine,
My candy costs more all the time.

Oh Mister Lawmaker, President too,
Please end this war and I'll give some to you,
To lose my big brother would sure be a crime,
My candy costs more all the time.

Some day I'll grow up and be me a man,
And there'll be free candy for kids in this land;
My brother will come home from that old front line,
And candy will always be mine.

He's Got The Whole World In His Hands

He's got the wind and the rain in His hands,
He's got the sun and the moon in His hands,
He's got the wind and the rain in His hands,
He's got the whole world in His hands.

He's got you and me, brother, in His hands,
He's got you and me, brother, in His hands,
He's got you and me, brother, in His hands,
He's got the whole world in His hands.

He's got the little bitty baby in His hands,
He's got the little bitty baby in His hands,
He's got the little bitty baby in His hands,
He's got the whole world in His hands.

He's got everybody in His hands,
He's got everybody in His hands,
He's got everybody in His hands,
He's got the whole world in His hands.

Repeat Verse One

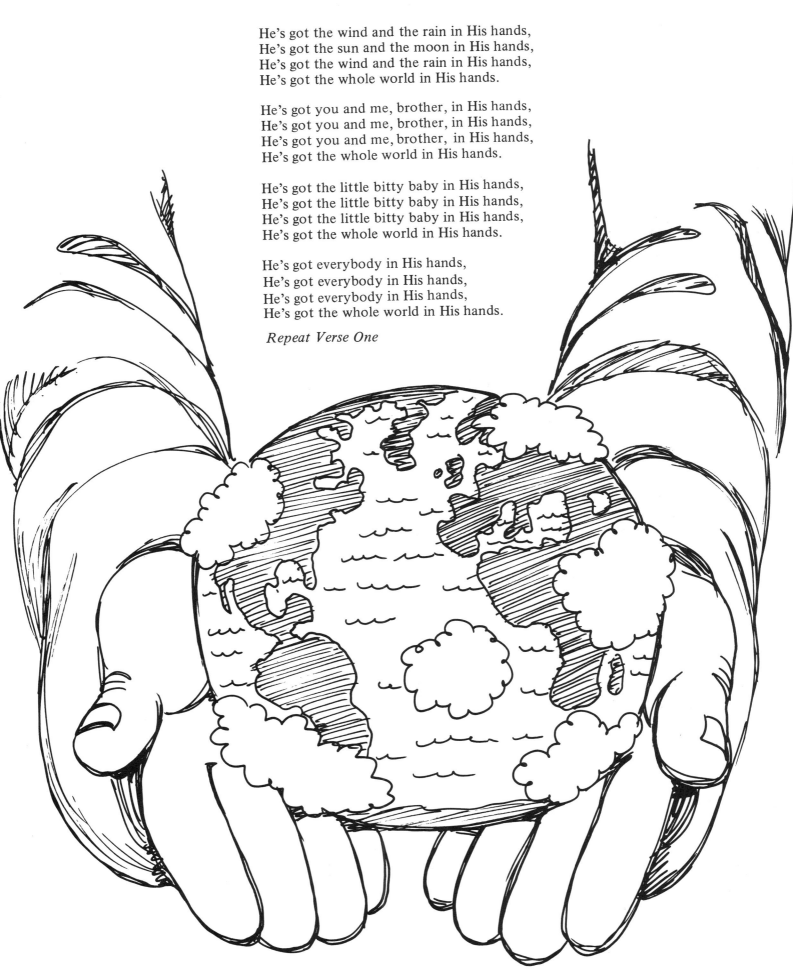

Simple Gifts

The Shakers, who made up this song, were a 19th-century religious sect known for their ingenious and beautiful crafts. They made their own furniture and tools, and lived simple, uncomplicated lives.

United Nations Make A Chain

This song was written in 1947, when the United Nations was a brand-new experiment and the memory of World War II was fresh in the people's minds.

U – nit – ed Na – tions make a chain, Ev – 'ry link is free – dom's name, Keep your hands on __ that plough, hold on. _____

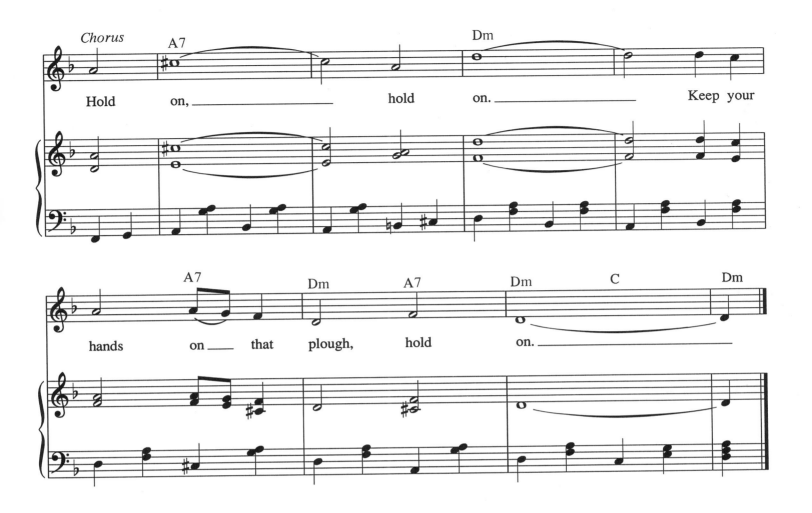

Now the war is over and done,
Let's keep the peace that we have won;
Keep your hand on that plow, hold on! *Chorus*

Freedom's name is mighty sweet;
Black and white are gonna meet;
Keep your hand on that plow, hold on! *Chorus*

Many men have fought and died
So we could be here side by side;
Keep your hand on that plow, hold on! *Chorus*

Oh, Freedom

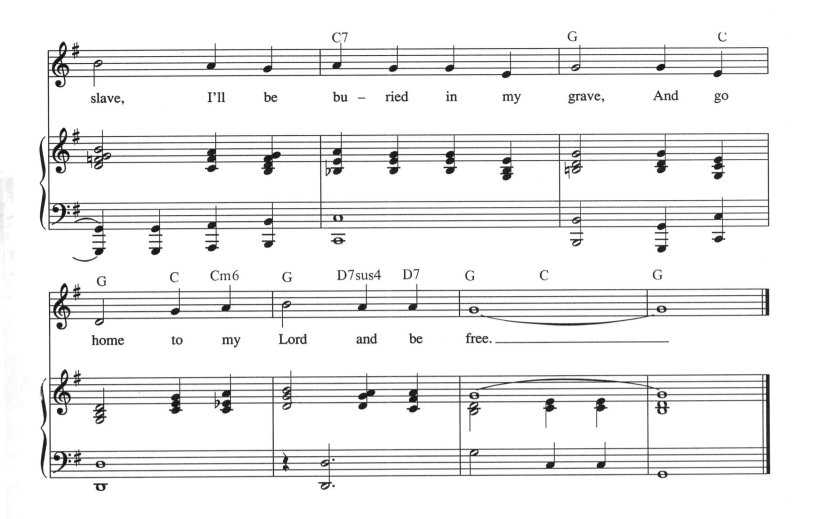

No more moaning, no more moaning,
No more moaning over me.
And before I'll be a slave,
I'll be buried in my grave,
And go home to my Lord and be free.

No more weeping. . .

There'll be singing. . .

Tenting on the Old Camp Ground

Walter Kittredge wrote this famous song in 1863, while preparing to answer a draft call to serve in the Union Army during the Civil War.

Words and Music by Walter Kittredge

We're tent – ing to – night on the old camp ground,
Give us a song to cheer Our wea – ry hearts, a
song of home And friends we love so dear.

Chorus
Man-y are the hearts that are wea-ry to-night, Wish-ing for the war to

We've been tenting tonight on the old camp ground,
Thinking of days gone by,
Of the loved ones at home that gave us the hand,
And the tear said, "Goodbye!" *Chorus*

We are tired of war on the old camp ground,
Many are dead and gone,
Of the brave and true who've left their homes,
Others been wounded long. *Chorus*

We've been fighting today on the old camp ground.
Many are lying near;
Some are dead and some are dying,
Many are in tears.

Final Chorus:
   Many are the hearts that are weary tonight,
   Wishing for the war to cease;
   Many are the hearts that are looking for the right
   To see the dawn of peace.
     Dying tonight, dying tonight,
     Dying on the old camp ground.

Vine and Fig Tree

2-part round

Ode To Joy

The "Ode to Joy" is sung in the finale of Beethoven's 9th Symphony — the "choral symphony."

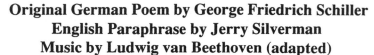

Original German Poem by George Friedrich Schiller
English Paraphrase by Jerry Silverman
Music by Ludwig van Beethoven (adapted)

Sing of joy from gods de – scend – ed, Daugh – ter of E –
Freu – de, schön – er Göt – ter fun – ken, Toch – ter aus E –

ly – si – um, Joy by love and hope at – ten – ded,
ly – si – um, Wir be – tre – ten feu – er – trun – ken,

Heav – en is your fair king–dom. For your mag – ic,
Himm – lisch – e, dein Heil – ig – thum. Dein – e zau – ber

The Whole Wide World Around

Bach used this chorale melody in his *St. Matthew Passion*. Because of its beauty and simplicity it is suitable for this hymn to peace.

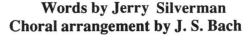

Words by Jerry Silverman
Choral arrangement by J. S. Bach

Like brothers and like sisters
We go our separate way;
Yet we must live together,
No matter come what may.
  We live here on this planet,
  We're rooted to its ground,
  We are the human family,
  The whole wide world around.

It is not always easy,
Each has his point of view.
And there are always conflicts,
We've lived through quite a few.
  Still hope does spring eternal,
  Our song it does resound.
  This hymn of peace will echo
  The whole wide world around.

Die Gedanken Sind Frei
Thoughts Are Free

German folk song
English translation
by Arthur Kevess

So I think as I please,
And this gives me pleasure,
My conscience decrees,
This right I must treasure;
My thoughts will not cater
To duke or dictator,
No man can deny
Die Gedanken sind frei!

And if tyrants take me
And throw me in prison,
My thoughts will burst free,
Like blossoms in season.
Foundations will crumble,
The structure will tumble,
And free men will cry
Die Gedanken sind frei!

Ich denke was ich will,
Und was mich beglücket,
Doch alles in der Still,
Und wie es sich schicket.
Mein Wunsch und Begehren
Kann niemand verwehren,
Es bleibet dabei:
Die Gedanken sind frei!

Und sperrt, man mich ein
Im finsteren Kerker,
Das alles sind rein
Vergebliche Werke;
Denn meine Gedanken
Zerreissen die Schranken
Und Mauern entzwei:
Die Gedanken sind frei!

When Johnny Comes Marching Home

The Civil War produced a great outpouring of song, unequalled in American history. This stirring theme of the returning soldier has been sung in all our wars since then.

Words and Music by Patrick S. Gilmore

When John – ny comes march – ing home a – gain, Hur – rah, _____ hur –

rah! _____ We'll give him a heart – y wel – come then, Hur – rah, _____ hur –

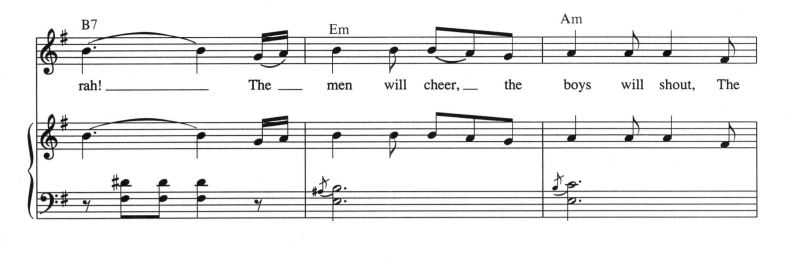

rah! _____ The ___ men will cheer, ___ the boys will shout, The

la — dies, they___ will all turn out, And we'll all feel

gay when John—ny comes march — ing home. _____

The old church bell will peal with joy,
  Hurrah, hurrah!
To welcome home our darling boy,
  Hurrah, hurrah!
The village lads and lassies say,
With roses they will strew the way,
And we'll all feel gay when Johnny comes
  marching home.

Get ready for the Jubilee,
  Hurrah, hurrah!
We'll give the hero three times three,
  Hurrah, hurrah!
The laurel wreath is ready now
To place upon his loyal brow,
And we'll all feel gay when Johnny comes
  marching home.

Let love and friendship on that day,
  Hurrah, hurrah!
Their choicest treasures then display,
  Hurrah, hurrah!
And let each one perform some part,
To fill with joy the warrior's heart,
And we'll all feel gay when Johnny comes
  marching home.

Shalom, Chaverim
Peace, Brothers

This is a round which may be sung in as many as eight parts. The Roman numerals indicate where the voices may enter. The Hebrew words simply mean: "Peace, brothers. . . till we meet again."

Israel

Sha - lom cha-ve-rim, sha - lom cha-ve-rim, Sha - lom, sha –

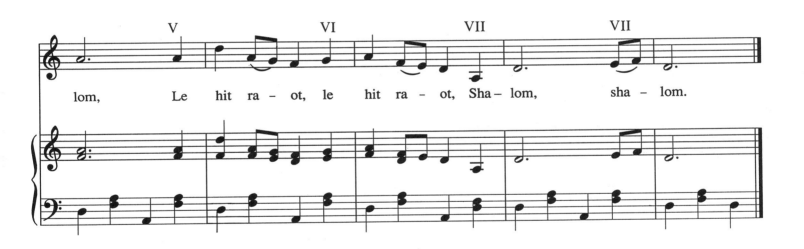

lom, Le hit ra - ot, le hit ra - ot, Sha - lom, sha - lom.

Go Down, Moses

During slavery times, the slaves sang of many heroes whose stories were told in the Bible. Perhaps none moved them more deeply than Moses, who led the children of Israel out of slavery.

Tell ol' Phar – aoh, To let my peo – ple go.

Thus saith the Lord, bold Moses said,
Let my people go,
If not, I'll smite your first-born dead,
Let my people go. *Chorus*

No more shall they in bondage toil…
Let them come out with Egypt's spoil… *Chorus*

The Lord told Moses what to do…
To lead the Hebrew children through… *Chorus*

O come along Moses, you'll not get lost…
Stretch out your rod and come across… *Chorus*

As Israel stood by the waterside…
At God's command it did divide… *Chorus*

When they reached the other shore…
They sang a song of triumph o'er… *Chorus*

Pharaoh said he'd go across…
But Pharaoh and his host were lost… *Chorus*

Jordan shall stand up like a wall,
And the walls of Jericho shall fall… *Chorus*

Your foes shall not before you stand…
And you'll possess fair Canaan's Land… *Chorus*

O let us all from bondage flee…
And let us all in Christ be free… *Chorus*

We need not always weep and mourn…
And wear these slavery chains forlorn… *Chorus*

Free At Last

. . . Yes, this will be the day when all of God's children, black men and white men, Jews and Gentiles, Protestants and Catholics, will be able to join hands all over this nation and sing in the words of the old Negro spiritual: "Free at last, free at last. Thank God Almighty, we are free at last." (*Martin Luther King, Jr., December 11, 1961.*)

On my knees when the light passed by,
I thank God I'm free at last,
Thought my soul would rise and fly,
I thank God I'm free at last. *Chorus*

Some of these mornings, bright and fair,
I thank God I'm free at last,
Gonna meet my Jesus in the middle of the air,
I thank God I'm free at last. *Chorus*

42

Kumbaya

Someone's singing, Lord, kumbaya,
Someone's singing, Lord, kumbaya,
Someone's singing, Lord, kumbaya,
Oh, Lord, kumbaya.

Someone's dancing, Lord, kumbaya,
Someone's dancing, Lord, kumbaya,
Someone's dancing, Lord, kumbaya,
Oh, Lord, kumbaya.

Someone's weeping, Lord, kumbaya,
Someone's weeping, Lord, kumbaya,
Someone's weeping, Lord, kumbaya,
Oh, Lord, kumbaya.

Someone's shouting, Lord, kumbaya,
Someone's shouting, Lord, kumbaya,
Someone's shouting, Lord, kumbaya,
Oh, Lord, kumbaya.

Someone's praying, Lord, kumbaya,
Someone's praying, Lord, kumbaya,
Someone's praying, Lord, kumbaya,
Oh, Lord, kumbaya.

Passing Through

Words and Music by Dick Blakeslee

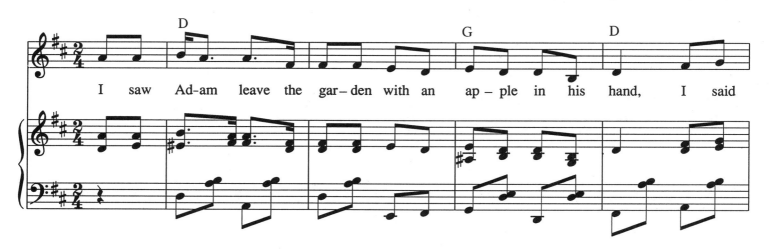

I saw Ad-am leave the gar-den with an ap-ple in his hand, I said

"Now you're out, what are you gon-na do?" _____ "Plant my crops and pray for

rain, May-be raise a lit-tle Cain, I'm an or-phan now and

I saw Jesus on the cross
On that hill called Calvary;
"Do you hate mankind for what they done to you?"
He said, "Talk of love, not hate,
Things to do - it's getting late.
I've so little time and I'm just passing through." *Chorus*

I shivered next to Washington
One night at Valley Forge,
"Why do the soldiers freeze here like they do?"
He said, "Men will suffer, fight,
Even die for what is right,
Even though they know they're only passing through." *Chorus*

Was at Franklin Roosevelt's side
Just a while before he died,
He said, "One world must come out of World War Two,
Yankee, Russian, white or tan,
Lord, a man is just a man,
We're all brothers and we're only passing through." *Chorus*

Bread And Roses

Although written in 1912 for a textile workers strike in Lowell, Massachusetts, this song speaks of a higher brotherhood and sisterhood among all people.

Music by Martha Coleman
Words by James Oppenhein

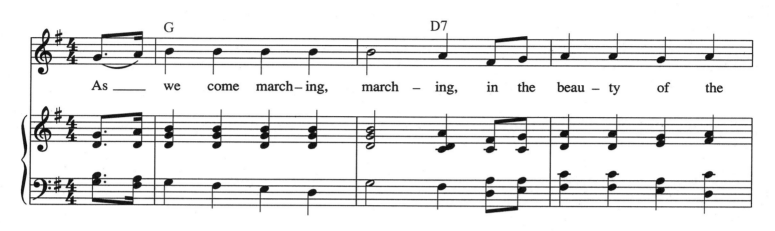

As ___ we come march–ing, march – ing, in the beau – ty of the

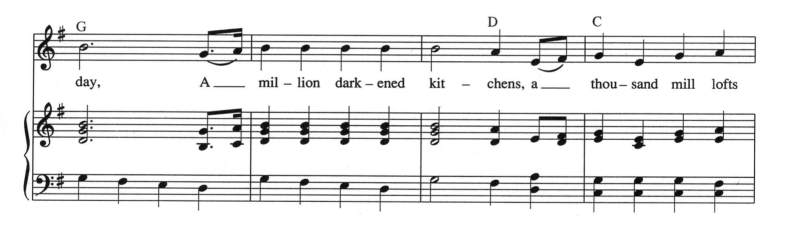

day, A ___ mil – lion dark – ened kit – chens, a ___ thou–sand mill lofts

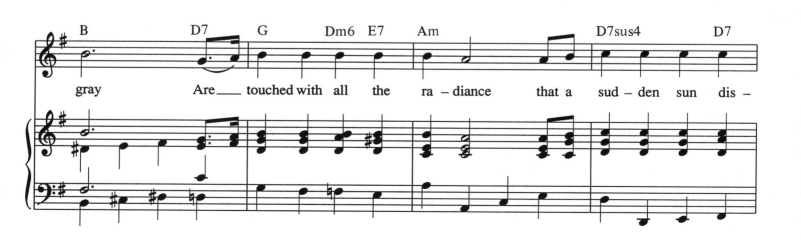

gray Are ___ touched with all the ra – diance that a sud – den sun dis –

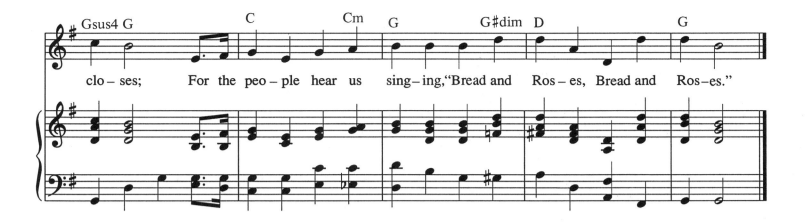

clo – ses;   For the peo – ple hear us   sing – ing, "Bread and   Ros – es, Bread and   Ros–es."

As we come marching, marching, we battle too, for men,
For they are women's children and we mother them again.
Our lives shall not be sweated from birth until life closes.
Hearts starve as well as bodies:
Give us bread, but give us roses.

As we come marching, marching, unnumbered women dead
Go crying through our singing their ancient song of bread.
Small art and love and beauty their drudging spirits knew.
Yes, it is bread that we fight for,
But we fight for roses, too.

As we come marching, marching, we bring the Greater Days,
The rising of the women means the rising of the race.
No more the drudge and idler, ten that toil where one reposes,
But a sharing of life's glories,
Bread and Roses, Bread and Roses.

Woke Up This Morning With My Mind On Freedom

This song is one of the many that came out of the civil rights movement of the 1960s.

Wade In The Water

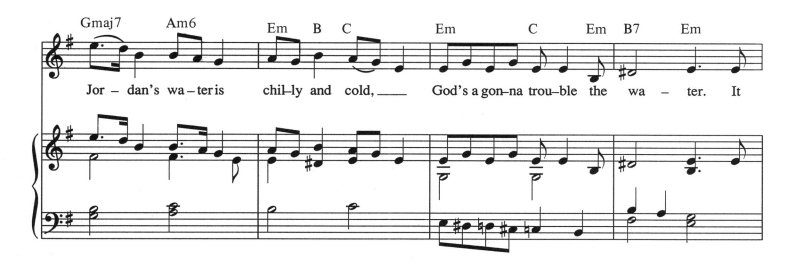

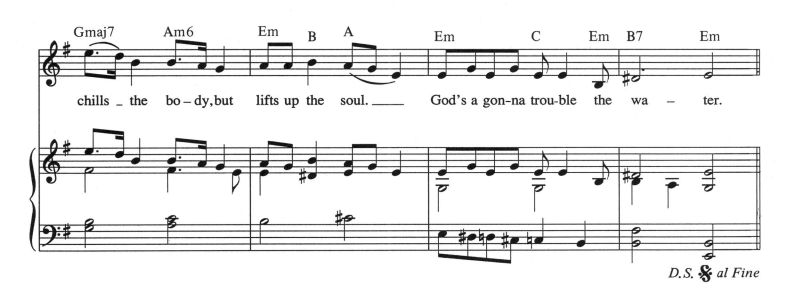

D.S. 𝄋 *al Fine*

If you get there before I do,
  God's a-gonna trouble the water,
Tell all my friends I'm coming too,
  God's a-gonna trouble the water. *Chorus*

Oh How Lovely Is The Evening

3-part round

The Family Of Man

By Fred Dallas

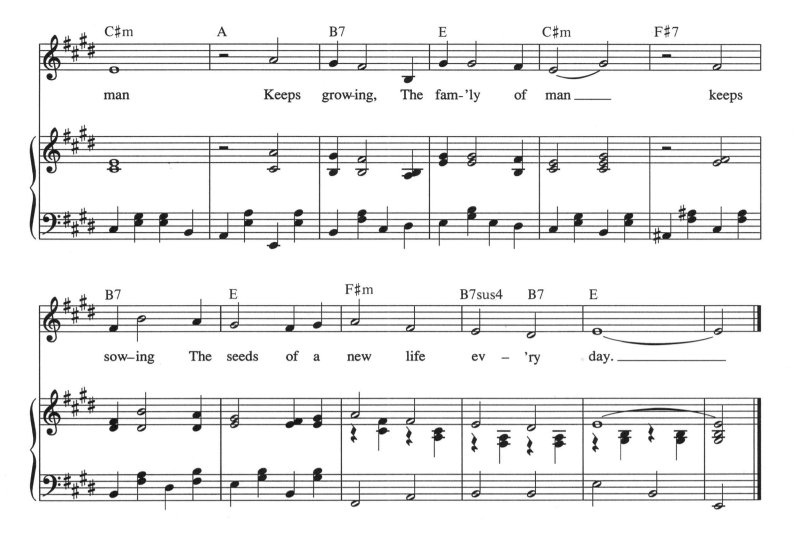

man   Keeps grow-ing,   The fam-'ly of man _____ keeps

sow—ing   The seeds of a new life ev — 'ry day. _____

I've got a sister in Melbourne a brother in Paree.
The whole world is dad and mother to me.
Wherever you turn you will find my kin
Whatever the creed, or the color of the skin. *Chorus*

The miner in the Rhondda, the coolie in Beijing,
Men across the world who reap and plough and spin.
They' ve all got a life and others to share it.
Let's bridge the oceans and declare it.   *Chorus*

From the North Pole ice to the snow at the other.
There isn't a man I wouldn't call brother.
But I haven't much time, I've had my fill
Of the men of war who want to kill. *Chorus*

Some people say the world is a horrible place.
But it's just good of bad as the human race:
Dirt and misery or health and joy.
Man can build or can destroy. *Chorus*

All My Trials

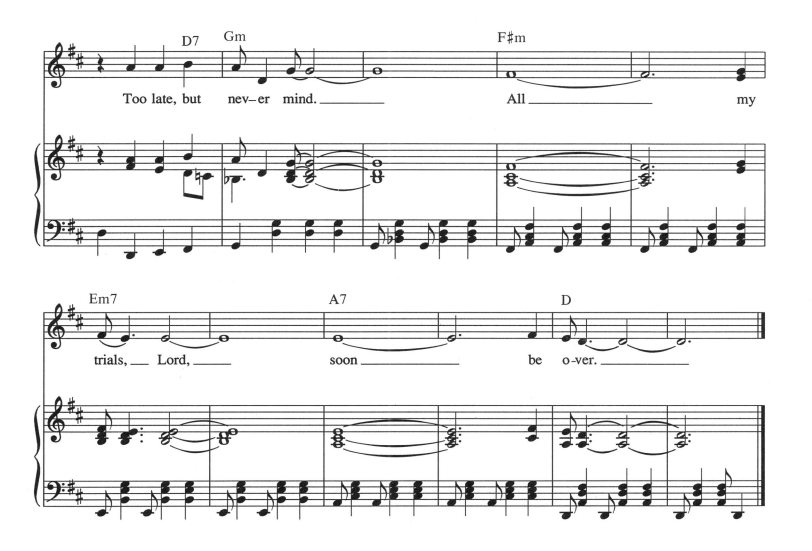

Hush little baby, don't you cry,
You know your daddy was born to die. *Chorus*

I had a little book, 'twas given to me,
And every page spelled "Victory." *Chorus*

Let Us Break Bread Together

Let us join hands together on our knees,
Let us join hands together on our knees.
When I fall on my knees with my face to the rising sun,
Oh, Lord have mercy if you please.

Let us love one another. . .

Let us all sing together. . .

We will all come together. . .

See how many verses you can make up.

Strangest Dream

Words and Music by Ed McCurdy

Last night I had the strang — est dream, I'd nev — er dreamed be — fore; _____ I dreamed the world had all a — greed to put an end to war. _____ I dreamed I saw a might — y room, The room was

And when the paper was all signed,
And a million copies made,
They all joined hands and bowed their heads,
And grateful prayers were prayed.
And the people in the streets below
Were dancing 'round and 'round,
While swords and guns and uniforms
Were scattered on the ground.

Repeat first 16 measures of first verse — ending on first beat of measure 16.

The Golden Rule

1st Verse & Music by George Levine
Additional Lyrics by Jerry Silverman

I'm not here to preach a ser–mon, but I've got a lot to say; This world must be u–nit–ed for to walk the right–eous way. It's time to learn a les–son that's thou–sands of years old: We've got to live by the Gold–en Rule and not the rule of gold. We've got to

Each bullet has a price tag, each A-bomb costs so much,
And they even make a profit on each wheelchair and each crutch.
Yes, it's the rule of gold that leaves the dying to the youth;
It's time our eyes were opened and we learned this simple truth. *Chorus*

So listen all you people, wherever you may be,
The world cries out for peace and friendship and democracy.
It's time to put an end to wars - you know just what I mean,
And live together side by side - and that's our golden dream. *Chorus*

I'm On My Way

I asked my brother to come with me,
I asked my brother to come with me,
I asked my brother to come with me,
I'm on my way, great God, I'm on my way.

If he says no, I'll go alone…

I asked my sister to go with me…

If she says no, I'll go alone…

I asked my boss to let me go…

If he says no, I'll go anyhow…

I'm on my way to Freedom land…